Cats Around the World

Written and Illustrated by
Ted Meyer

Published by:

Santa Monica Press LLC
P.O. Box 1076
Santa Monica, CA 90406-1076
1 800-784-9553
www.santamonicapress.com
books@santamonicapress.com

Printed in China

Santa Monica Press books are available at special quantity discounts when purchased in bulk by corporations, organizations, or groups. Please call our Special Sales department at 1-800-784-9553.

Library of Congress Cataloging-in-Publication Data

Meyer, Ted.
Cats Around the World / written & illustrated by Ted Meyer.
    p. cm.

ISBN 1-891661-34-5
1. Cats--Humor. I. Title.

PN6231.C23 M49 2003
714.5'973--dc21

2003017602

To Dr. Moore:
Savior of Animals,
BIG and small.

From Outer Space,
you just have to wonder:
Where are all the cats?

Serbia and Montenegro

Serbia and Montenegro

Adriatic Sea

Macedonia

Albania

In Albanian, Cat = Mace

Italy

Greece

There are no cats in Antarctica.

NORTH AMERICA

ATLANTIC OCEAN

PACIFIC OCEAN

SOUTH AMERICA

ARGENTINA

In Spanish,
Cat = Gato

PACIFIC
OCEAN

INDIAN
OCEAN

AUSTRALIA

They
speak
English
in
Australia.

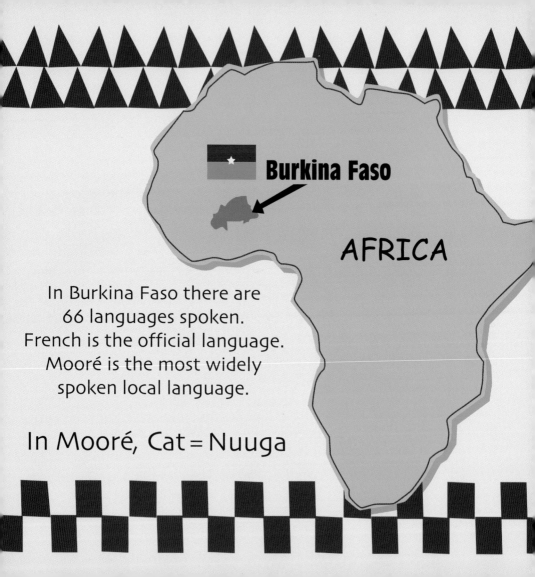

Burkina Faso

AFRICA

In Burkina Faso there are
66 languages spoken.
French is the official language.
Mooré is the most widely
spoken local language.

In Mooré, Cat = Nuuga

BRAZIL

PACIFIC
OCEAN

ATLANTIC
OCEAN

Rio de Janeiro

In Brazil
they speak
Portuguese.

Cat = Gato

Canada

In Canada they speak French and English.

PACIFIC OCEAN

South America

Chile

Easter Island is part of Chile.

Cats are not native to the island so there is no native word for Cat.

Santiago

In

China

Cat is 猫

(pronounced Mao)

Cats are credited
with the power
to scare off evil spirits.

Beijing

Shanghai

When you visit

Costa Rica,

people ask you,
"Have you seen any Iguanas?"

They never ask you about cats.

Cat = Gato

Florida
USA

Havana

CUBA

In Spanish,
Cat is **Gato**

Arabic is spoken in

Egypt

Cat = Qeta

Bast (or Bastet) is an Egyptian goddess with the body of a woman and the head of a cat. She is the daughter of the Sun God and she is the protectress of women; mothers and children; and goddess of music, dance, family, sunrise, and pleasure.

ENGLAND

The British Shorthair, probably the oldest English breed of cat, traces its ancestry back to the domestic cats of Rome. This breed was first prized for its physical strength and hunting ability.

In Finland
Cat
is
Kissa.

France

Cat = Chat

GERMANY

Cat = Katze

In
Greece,
Cat is

ΓΑΤΑ
(pronounced Gata for female)

ΓΑΤΟΣ
(pronounced Gatos for male)

Guatemala

In Mayan art, on wall and cave murals,
and on vases, the jaguar
is sometimes shown in both its
naturally occurring colors:
Black (the jaguar god of the underworld) or
Light (the jaguar god of the upperworld).

In Central America
they speak Spanish.

Cat = Gato

India

In India most people speak
Urdu, Hindi, or English.

In Urdu, Cat = بِلّی
(pronounced Bill-ly)

In Hindi, Cat = बिल्ली
(pronounced Bill-ly)

Iran

In Iran they speak Farsi.

Cat = گربه

(pronounced Gorbé)

Persian Cats come from Iran.

Ireland

In both
Gaelic & English,
a Cat is a Cat.

The Isle of Man

The Manx Cat,
a tailless breed, comes
from the Isle of Man.

A Manx can
have a full tail,
a short tail, or
no tail at all.

Northern
Ireland

Ireland

England

London

שראל

ISRAEL

Israel → Syria
Iraq

Egypt   Saudi
Arabia

AFRICA

In Hebrew
cat is written

חתול

(pronounced Chatool)

ISRAEL

FELIS CARACAL

0.18   ישראל

Switzerland Austria Hunga

France

Slovenia

Croatia

Italy

Bosnia &
Herzegovir

ROME
★

SARDINIA

In Italian,
Cat = Gatto

SICILY

In Jamaica, Cat is Cat.

 Cuba

Jamaica

Mexico

Kingston ★ Haiti

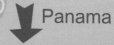 Panama

In Japan,

猫

spells Cat.
(pronounced Neko)

North Korea

IN KOREAN, CAT IS WRITTEN

(pronounced Ko-yang-yi)

South Korea

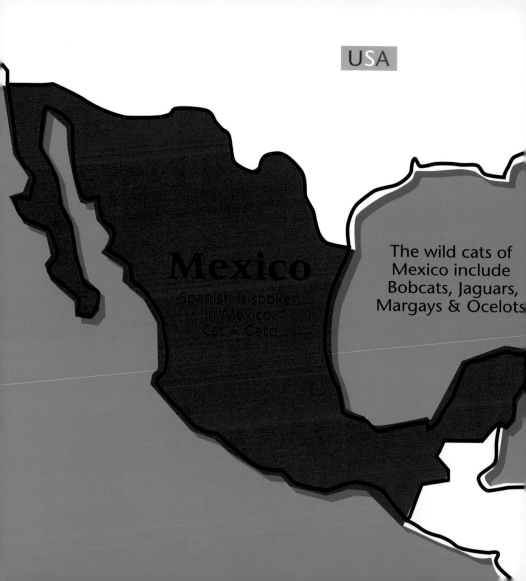

USA

Mexico

Spanish is spoken
in Mexico.
Cat = Gato

The wild cats of
Mexico include
Bobcats, Jaguars,
Margays & Ocelots

Morocco

In Arabic,
cat = قطة

(pronounced Ghat)

kingdom of Nepal

In most of Nepal they speak Nepali.
Cat = Biralo

But in the mountains they speak Sherpa.
Cat = Bänmang

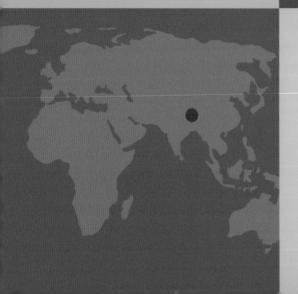

The Netherlands

In Dutch,
Cat = Kat

New Zealand

In New Zealand they speak English and Maori.

In Maori, Cat = Ngeru

Nor way

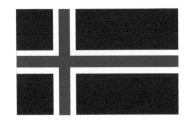

Cat is Katt

Norwegian Forest Cats are the largest domestic breed. They explored the world with the Vikings, protecting their grain stores on land and sea.

Papua New Guinea

Cat = Pusi

Papua New Guinea has over 700 languages.
This is just one translation.
Not all languages have a word for cat.

Яussia

Cat = Ko

The Russian Blue is a descendant of the
Royal Cats of the Russian Czars
and was a favored pet of Queen Victoria.
Another breed, the Siberian, is the national cat of Russia.

Saudi Arabia

Syria
Jordan
Iraq

MECCA

Yeme

In Arabic,
cat is

قط

(pronounced Ghat)

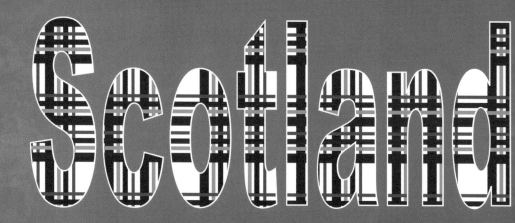

Scotland

Scottish Folds have folded ears

THE FIRST KNOWN
SCOTTISH FOLD
CAT WAS SPOTTED
AT A FARM IN SCOTLAND.
HER NAME WAS SUSIE.

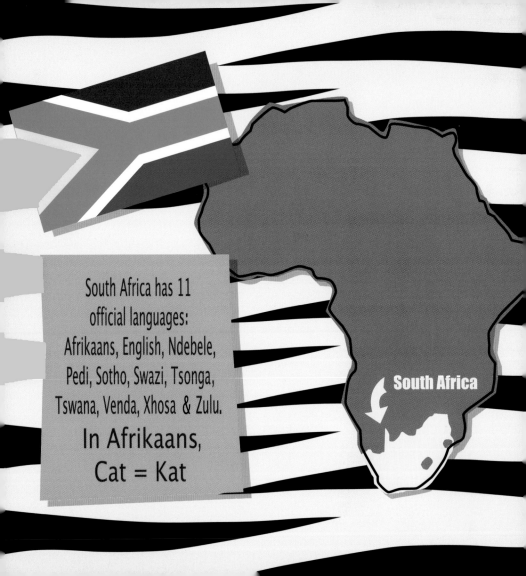

South Africa has 11
official languages:
Afrikaans, English, Ndebele,
Pedi, Sotho, Swazi, Tsonga,
Tswana, Venda, Xhosa & Zulu.

In Afrikaans,
Cat = Kat

South Africa

In Spanish,
Cat = Gato

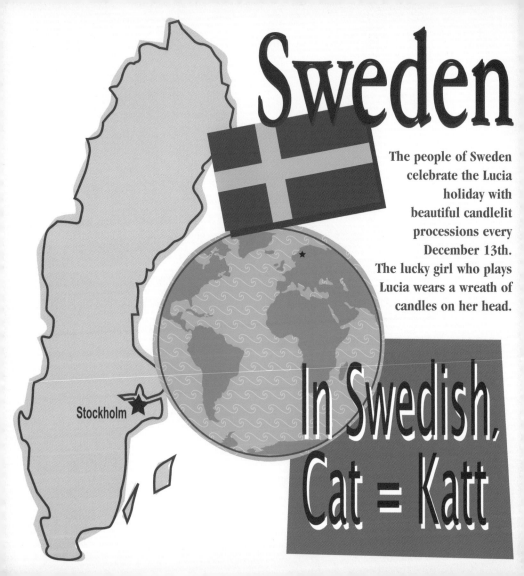

Sweden

The people of Sweden celebrate the Lucia holiday with beautiful candlelit processions every December 13th. The lucky girl who plays Lucia wears a wreath of candles on her head.

Stockholm

In Swedish, Cat = Katt

German

Cat = Katze

French

Cat = Chat

Switzerland

In Switzerland they speak 4 different languages.

Italian

Cat = Gatto

Romansh

Cat = Gat or Giat

Thailand

In Thai, Cat = แมว
(pronounced Meow)

The first Siamese cats to appear in the West were a gift from Siam (now Thailand) to the British ambassador (who brought them home to England).

United States

There are presently an estimated
53 million domestic cats in the U.S.A.

With so many cats on

The Earth,

you can only wonder how
many cats there are on

The Moon.

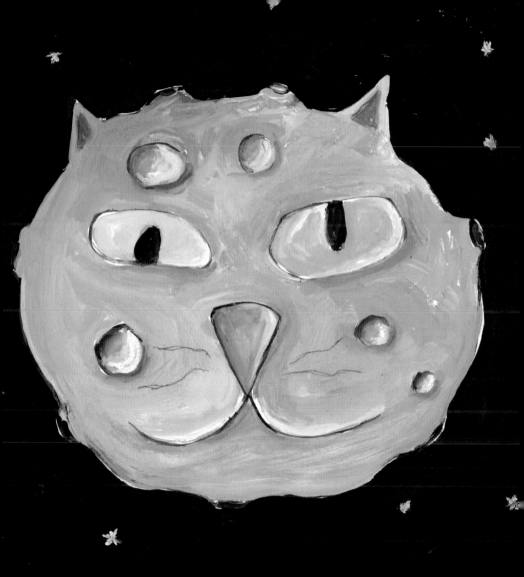

The End